THIS LAND CALLED AMERICA: **WASHINGTON**

CREATIVE EDUCATION

Published by Creative Education
P.O. Box 227, Mankato, Minnesota 56002
Creative Education is an imprint of The Creative Company
www.thecreativecompany.us

Design by Blue Design (www.bluedes.com)
Art direction by Rita Marshall
Book production by The Design Lab
Printed in the United States of America

Photographs by Alamy (Cephas Picture Library, Danita Delimont, D. Hurst,
Chris Luneski, Darren Newbery, Kevin Schafer), Corbis (Christie's Images,
Dave Bartruff, Inc., Lynn Goldsmith, Hulton-Deutsch Collection, Chase
Jarvis, Bob Krist, David Muench, Museum of History and Industry, PEMCO-
Webster & Stevens Collection/Museum of History and Industry, Seattle;
Louie Psihoyos, Connie Ricca, Joel W. Rogers, Galen Rowell, Steve Terrill,
Craig Tuttle, Stuart Westmorland), Getty Images (GABRIEL BOUYS/AFP,
MPI), iStockphoto

Library of Congress Cataloging-in-Publication Data
Washington / by Melissa Gish.
p. cm. — (This land called America)
Includes bibliographical references and index.
ISBN 978-1-58341-800-0
1. Washington (State)—Juvenile literature. I. Title. II. Series.
F891.3.G57 2009
979.7—dc22   2008009528

First Edition
9 8 7 6 5 4 3 2 1

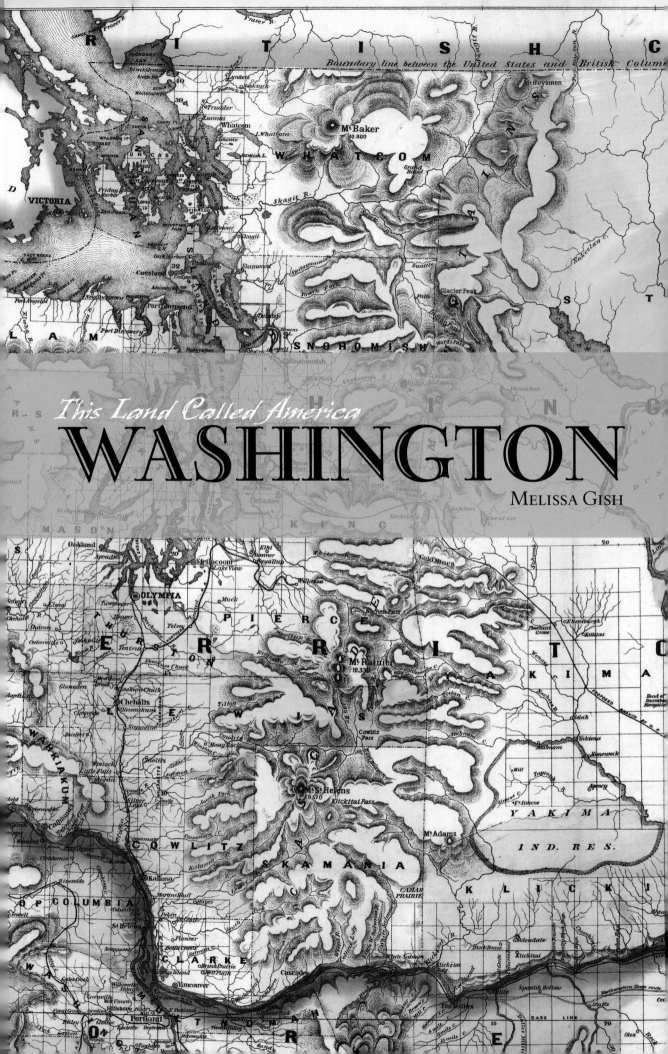

This Land Called America

WASHINGTON

Melissa Gish

THIS LAND CALLED AMERICA

Washington

MELISSA GISH

WESTERN WASHINGTON'S FAMOUS WINTER
DRIZZLES HAVE MELTED INTO SUNNY SUMMER.
NATURE LOVERS STAND PERCHED AT THE RAIL OF
A SMALL CRUISE SHIP. THEY HAVE COME FROM ALL
OVER THE COUNTRY TO THE SAN JUAN ISLANDS.
THE WATERS AROUND THE ISLANDS ARE HOME
TO ORCAS, OR KILLER WHALES. THESE HUGE
MARINE MAMMALS LEAP FROM THE SEA AS IF TO
GREET THE VISITORS. HARBOR SEALS AND TUFTED
PUFFINS ALSO APPEAR. LATER, A FERRY TAKES THE
TOURISTS BACK TO THE MAINLAND. THE SMELL OF
FRESHLY STEAMED SEAFOOD AND THE SOUND OF
MUSIC FILL THE AIR. IT'S TIME FOR MORE FUN AS
THE SUN GOES DOWN IN WASHINGTON.

YEAR

1775

EVENT

Spaniard Bruno Heceta and his crew are the first Europeans to set foot in Washington.

- 5 -

Northwest Bounty

Sir Francis Drake may have been the first European explorer to see the land now called Washington. That was in 1579. The first map of the area was made 200 years later by Spanish explorer Juan Perez. He sailed along Washington's coast in 1774, and more Spaniards followed the next year.

A few years later, English explorer James Cook sailed to Washington. He discovered a land teeming with wildlife. English traders soon flocked to the region looking for sea otter pelts, which were especially prized in Europe. Washington's American Indians were expert trappers. They traded the pelts for blankets, tools, and copper to make jewelry.

By the mid-18th century, too few otters were left to trap, and fur trading declined. But Washington had more to offer. American explorers Meriwether Lewis and William Clark discovered the land's bounty. In 1805, they mapped an overland trail across Washington to the Pacific Ocean. Pioneers soon followed them.

The new settlers encountered many American Indians. Among the tribes were the Chinook, Makah, and Nez Perce. These tribes relied on trapping, salmon fishing, and whale hunting for food. Some tribes carved

Lewis and Clark traveled with American Indian interpreters and guides (opposite) who taught them survival skills such as spearfishing (pictured).

YEAR
1792   American explorer Robert Gray discovers the mouth of the Columbia River, which he names after his ship.
EVENT

- 7 -

By the late 1800s, Seattle's waterfront was filled with sawmills, and leftover cut logs were used to build wharves along the shore.

State bird: willow goldfinch

Seattle sawmill, 1878

wooden totem poles and masks. Some lived in huts made of cattails. Others lived in "big houses," or wooden homes decorated with woodcarvings and paintings.

In 1848, the Oregon Territory was formed. The present states of Oregon, Idaho, Washington, and parts of Montana and Wyoming were included in this territory. Five years later, the northern half of this area split off and became the Washington Territory. Thousands of settlers arrived, having heard about the territory's fish-filled streams, rich soil, and abundant forests.

When white settlers took land from the American Indians, conflicts occurred. Despite this, the United States government wanted white settlement to expand. By the mid-1800s, most American Indians had been forced onto reservations, or lands that were set aside for them. But soon gold was discovered on the reservations. White miners took over that land as well, and the Indians had to move again.

Many people, including farmers, loggers, and factory owners, arrived in Washington to claim the area's resources. Year after year, Washington's rainy climate brought farmers bumper crops of wheat. Flour mills sprang up all over the territory.

The logging industry grew as well. In 1881, a man named John Dolbeer invented the donkey engine. This machine

YEAR
1805   Explorers Meriwether Lewis and William Clark enter the land that is now Washington.
EVENT

Many heavy donkey engines were abandoned in forests and can be found rusting by today's hikers.

changed the way trees were logged. Up until then, logging had to be done near rivers so that the heavy logs could be floated to sawmills or roads. The steam-powered donkey engine used ropes and cables to drag heavy logs up steep mountainsides to roads. That made it possible to log more forestland.

On November 11, 1889, Washington became the 42nd state. Two years later, the U.S. Navy created a shipyard in Bremerton. There, ships could be dry-docked. When a ship is dry-docked, it is sailed into a docking area, and then the water is pumped out so the ship can be repaired in a dry place. Battleships such as the USS *Iowa* were dry-docked at Bremerton.

In 1899, Washington's first hydroelectric plant was built at Snoqualmie Falls. It used the energy created by water falling over a dam on the Snoqualmie River to create electricity. As Washington entered the 20th century, this power aided in the continued growth of industry and agriculture in the state.

The first diesel-powered ships were built in Bremerton in 1914 and were often nearly 100 feet (30 m) long.

YEAR

1833 Pioneer John Ball becomes Washington's first teacher while living at Fort Vancouver for a year.

EVENT

- *10* -

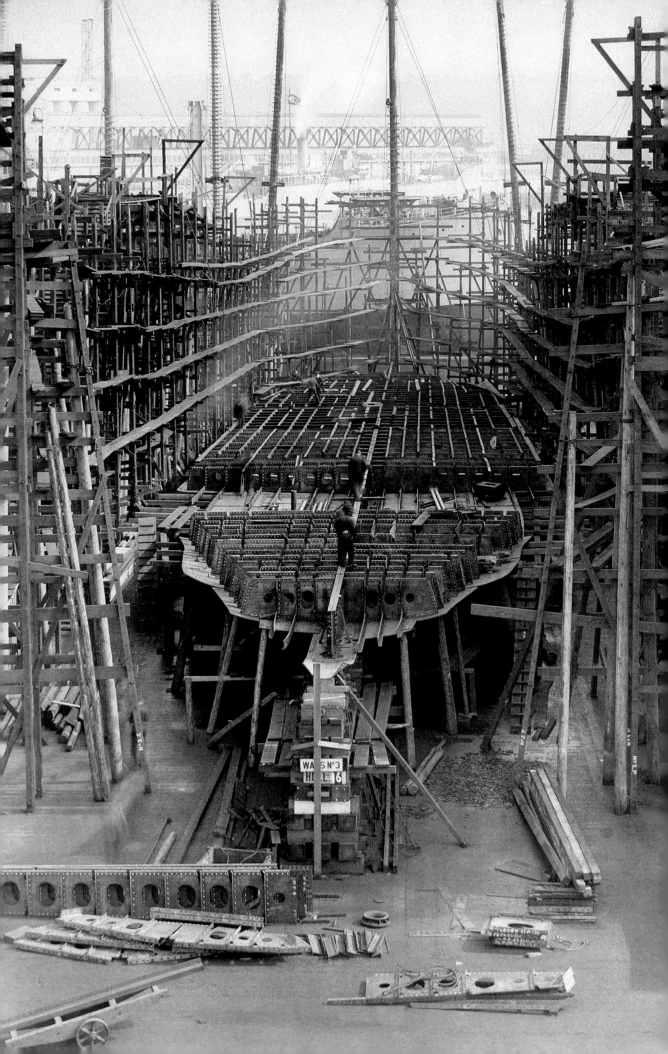

Fire and Ice

THE STATE OF WASHINGTON IS LOCATED IN AMERICA'S NORTHWEST. THE COLUMBIA RIVER SEPARATES THE EASTERN THIRD OF WASHINGTON FROM THE REST OF THE STATE. THE RIVER STARTS IN CANADA, WHICH BORDERS WASHINGTON TO THE NORTH. AT WASHINGTON'S SOUTHERN BORDER, THE RIVER TURNS WEST. IT SEPARATES WASHINGTON AND OREGON, EMPTYING INTO THE

Pacific Ocean. Washington's entire western side touches the Pacific Ocean. The state's neighbor to the east is Idaho.

The mighty Columbia feeds hundreds of smaller rivers, tributaries, and streams throughout the Columbia River Basin. The river has more than a dozen dams in Canada and the U.S. The Grand Coulee Dam was built in 1942. It created Roosevelt Lake in northeastern Washington. Fishermen love this remote area. Rainbow trout and kokanee salmon are put into the lake every year just so people can try to catch them. Moose, elk, and mule deer make their homes around the lake.

West of the Columbia River, the Cascade Range extends from Canada to northern California. In Washington, most mountains are 4,500 to 5,000 feet (1,370–1,525 m) high, but Mt. Rainier is much higher than the rest. This mountain, the tallest in the Cascade Range and the highest point in the state, stands 14,410 feet (4,392 m) tall. Like many of Washington's mountains, Mt. Rainier is an active volcano.

Kokanee salmon, sockeye salmon that live in lakes rather than rivers, are usually less than 20 inches (51 cm) long.

Approximately two million people visit Mt. Rainier and its forested national park each year.

YEAR

1851   American pioneers establish the first settlement in present-day Seattle.

EVENT

Another active volcano in Washington is Mount St. Helens in the Cascades. In 1980, the top of the mountain exploded. Molten lava poured out. Burning ash flew high into the air. Fifty-seven people were killed. Large areas of forestland were destroyed, and many animals died.

To the west of the Cascades, the Pacific Coast is dotted with harbors for fishing boats. Crabs, sturgeon, salmon, and rockfish are common catches. Estuaries, or places where freshwater rivers empty into the sea, are important locations for oyster farming.

The Puget Sound area on the Pacific Coast looks like pieces of a jigsaw puzzle. The land is cut by numerous channels and inlets. There are many wetland areas and islands. Most of these places have been developed with homes and businesses.

YEAR

1871

EVENT

The San Juan Islands, in upper Puget Sound, are declared to be part of Washington instead of Canada.

Across Puget Sound is a large piece of land called the Olympic Peninsula. It is surrounded by water on three sides. This area has one of the wettest climates in America. Every year, 12 to 14 feet (3.7–4.3 m) of rain falls. This moisture feeds the only rainforests in North America. There, Sitka spruce and western hemlock trees grow to enormous sizes. They can reach 300 feet (91 m) tall and 23 feet (7 m) around. The largest portion of rainforest is protected in Olympic National Park.

Between the Pacific Ocean and the Cascades, winter snow is rare in Washington, except in high, flat areas and on mountaintops. The ocean breeze often keeps the temperature above freezing, but rain falls nearly every day. Summers are much drier, with sunshine and pleasant temperatures.

East of the Cascades, winters are much harsher. Heavy snow blankets the land, and winds can blow up to 50 miles (80 km) per hour. Summers are warm, and rain falls lightly, making the eastern part of Washington a great place to grow crops such as apples. Washington provides half of America's apples. Sweet onions, berries, grapes, and wheat are also top crops.

In the agricultural region of eastern Washington called the Palouse, wheat is harvested in early August.

Much of the Olympic Peninsula's land is set aside for conservation and environmental study.

Technology and Taste

TODAY, ABOUT THREE-QUARTERS OF WASHINGTON'S POPULATION IS WHITE. JUST UNDER 10 PERCENT OF THE STATE'S PEOPLE ARE HISPANIC OR LATINO. ASIAN AMERICAN AND AFRICAN AMERICAN PEOPLE TOGETHER MAKE UP ABOUT 10 PERCENT OF THE POPULATION. LESS THAN TWO PERCENT OF THE STATE'S POPULATION IS AMERICAN

Indian. Roughly half of the Indians in Washington still live on or near reservations.

Bill Gates established the Bill & Melinda Gates Foundation to help fund schools and health research programs.

Most of Washington's Indian reservations are located in rural areas, far from big cities. But Washington's biggest city, Seattle, is the hometown of the third-richest person in the world: Bill Gates. He is the founder of Microsoft, the world's largest computer company. Microsoft is headquartered in Redmond, Washington, where the company continues to expand across almost 400 acres (162 ha). Microsoft employs thousands of people who work on everything from software design to new product development.

The oldest farmers market in the U.S., which celebrated its centennial in 2007, can be found in Seattle.

YEAR

1909 Washington hosts a World's Fair called the Alaska-Yukon-Pacific Exposition in Seattle.

EVENT

Seattle native Jimi Hendrix combined the sounds of blues, rock, and jazz to create his unique style.

In addition to supporting a major computer industry, Seattle offers a strong musical tradition. Judy Collins and Jimi Hendrix, musical greats of the 1960s, were both born in Seattle. A style of music called grunge was also created in Seattle. It was made popular by the Seattle bands Pearl Jam and Soundgarden and by Kurt Cobain and his band Nirvana.

Seattle's sister city Tacoma was the hometown of Bing Crosby. He was a famous singer and actor from the 1930s until his death in 1977. One of his best-loved movies, *White Christmas*, can be seen on television every winter.

Along with its music, Seattle is also known for its coffee. In 1971, three friends—Jerry Baldwin, Zev Siegel, and Gordon Bowker—decided to start a business together. They opened a coffee roasting company and called it Starbucks. Since

From its start in Seattle, Starbucks has expanded into more than 15,000 locations in 44 countries.

YEAR

1917   Named after Meriwether Lewis, Fort Lewis military base is established in the Puget Sound area.

EVENT

Howard Schultz joined the company in 1982, Starbucks has become the largest coffeehouse company in the world.

The world's largest aircraft builder is also located in Seattle. In 1910, William E. Boeing bought a shipyard in Seattle. But he did not want to build ships. He wanted to build airplanes. In 1916, Boeing opened America's first airplane factory. Today, Boeing's main assembly building, which is located in Everett, Washington, is considered to be the world's largest building with the largest amount of usable space.

With so many forests in Washington, logging has remained a top industry. Washington is America's second-largest producer of lumber (after Oregon). Coal mining was once a big industry, but now drilling for oil and natural gas is more important. Exploring for these resources causes controversy, though, as some people fear that drilling will damage Washington's environment.

From the manufacturing of aircraft (opposite) to the production of lumber from logging (above), Washington's industries are strong and diverse.

YEAR

1942   The Columbia River's Grand Coulee Dam, the largest concrete structure in the U.S., is completed.

EVENT

W inemaking also provides jobs and profits for Washington. The state ranks second (behind California) in winemaking in America. Nearly 600 wineries are located in Washington, and about 120,000 tons (109,000 t) of grapes are harvested each year. Many wineries conduct tours for visitors.

Wineries are not the only attractions for visitors to Washington. Tourism has become a major industry across the state. Hotels in the mountains offer skiing and hiking adventures. Resorts on the Pacific coast offer fishing and sailing. Washington shares its tourism industry with the neighboring Canadian city of Vancouver, British Columbia. Whale-watching tours and cruise ships travel between Vancouver and Washington. And because Vancouver is the host of the 2010 Winter Olympic Games, Washington will likely benefit from the added tourism in the area.

Summer wines (above) from vineyards along the state's river valleys and winter powder (opposite) in its mountains draw visitors to Washington to chill and thrill in the Pacific Northwest.

Wonderful Washington

WASHINGTON IS A UNIQUE STATE. IT IS THE ONLY STATE NAMED AFTER A U.S. PRESIDENT. IT ALSO HAS THE ONLY STATE FLAG WITH A PRESIDENT'S PICTURE ON IT. WASHINGTON'S HISTORICAL SITES, WILD LANDS, AND BUSTLING CITY LIFE ALSO SET IT APART.

Fort Vancouver is a national historic site on the Washington-Oregon border. In 1825, the fort became an important fur-trading post. Today, with restored houses, a watchtower, store, and fur storage building, the fort looks as it may have appeared almost 200 years ago.

A more recent chapter in history is featured at the American Museum of Radio and Electricity in Bellingham. There, a life-sized model of the famous ship *Titanic*'s radio room is on display. Visitors to the museum can also see many radio, telegraph, and lighting devices, including some early light bulbs from American inventor Thomas Edison's laboratory.

Washington's wilderness areas also draw in visitors. The state's mountains and forests lure adventurers outdoors to ski, hike, hunt, and fish. Mt. Rainier offers climbers an icy challenge. Avalanches are common, and the weather can change quickly. Only about half the people who try to climb Mt. Rainier make it to the top.

Fort Vancouver (opposite) is an interesting place for history buffs, but adventure seekers take to Mt. Rainier's steep slopes (pictured).

Spokane hosts a World's Fair with an environmental theme: "Celebrating Tomorrow's Fresh New Environment."

While some people ski and climb Washington's mountains, others search the hills for money. In 1971, a man known by the fake name D. B. Cooper hijacked an airplane for $200,000. After he got the money, he parachuted out of the plane over the mountains near Oregon. Cooper disappeared, but people believe the money might still be in Washington's forests.

People looking to spend money instead of find it come from all over the world to shop at Pike Place Market in downtown Seattle. There, farmers and fishermen sell fruits, vegetables, and seafood. In addition, artists, craftspeople, and musicians fill every corner of the market.

Fish fly through the air in Pike Place Market. Instead of handing fish to each other, workers at Sol Amon's Pure Food & Fish throw fresh fish across their fish stand. The workers sing and tell stories, too.

Those looking to see more of Seattle can get a view of the entire city from atop the world-famous Space Needle. This 605-foot-tall (184 m) tower was built in 1962, when Seattle hosted a World's Fair. Near the top of the tower is a 138-foot-wide (42 m) saucer with an outdoor observation deck. The saucer slowly turns in a complete circle every 47 minutes.

In Seattle, everything is fresh, from the seafood and produce at Pike Place Market (above) to the air atop the Space Needle (opposite).

YEAR
1990   The city of SeaTac, surrounding and named for the Seattle-Tacoma International Airport, is established.
EVENT

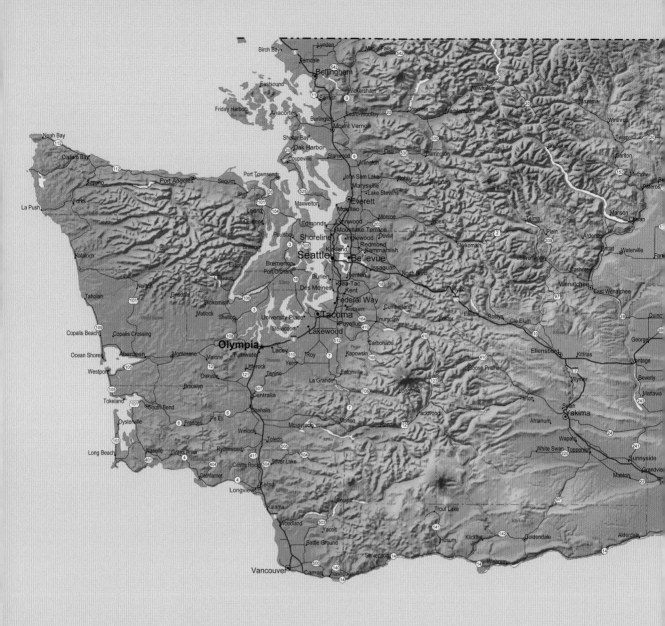

QUICK FACTS

Population: 6,468,424

Largest city: Seattle (pop. 594,210)

Capital: Olympia

Entered the union: November 11, 1889

Nickname: Evergreen State

State flower: coast rhododendron

State bird: willow goldfinch

Size: 71,300 sq mi (184,666 sq km)—18th-biggest in U.S.

Major industries: aircraft manufacturing, computer software, logging, tourism

The view from atop the Space Needle includes Safeco Field, where Major League Baseball's Mariners play. The National Football League's Seahawks also call Seattle home. Until 2008, Washington's men's and women's pro basketball teams, the SuperSonics and the Storm, played at KeyArena in downtown Seattle. The SuperSonics , who moved to Oklahoma City in 2008, had a unique mascot. Its name was Squatch. This is short for "Sasquatch," who is also known as Bigfoot. Bigfoot is a mysterious, apelike creature of Pacific Northwest legends.

Washington is a wonderful example of the beauty to be found in the Pacific Northwest. It is a place where people can breathe clean mountain air and enjoy the salty spray of the Pacific Ocean. Folks are friendly and care about the environment, and they work hard to help their cities grow. But they also strive to keep the many natural resources of "The Evergreen State" safe for the future.

YEAR

2000   President Bill Clinton signs a law making Hanford Reach, a portion of the Columbia River, a national monument.

EVENT

BIBLIOGRAPHY

Jarvela, Angela. *The Washington Almanac.* Portland, Ore.: Westwinds Press, 2003.

Lloyd, Tanya. *Washington.* North Vancouver, British Columbia: Whitecap Books, 2005.

Lucas, Eric. *Hidden Washington.* Berkeley, Calif.: Ulysses Press, 2007.

Peterson, Brenda. *Pacific Northwest: Land of Light and Water.* Seattle: Sasquatch Books, 2002.

Washington Secretary of State. "Washington History." State of Washington. http://www.secstate.wa.gov/history.

INDEX

American Indians 7, 9, 18–19

American Museum of Radio and Electricity 27

animals 5, 7, 13, 14

Boeing, William E. 23

border states 12

Crosby, Bing 20

Dolbeer, John 9–10

explorers and traders 6–7

Fort Vancouver 27

Gates, Bill 19

industries 9, 10, 14, 17, 23, 24

   aircraft manufacturing 23

   farming 9, 17

   fishing 14

   logging 9, 10, 23

   tourism 24

   winemaking 24

land regions and features 9, 10, 12, 13–14, 17, 23, 27, 28

   forests 9, 14, 17, 23, 27, 28

   highest point 13

   lakes and rivers 10, 12, 13

mountains 13, 14, 17, 27, 28

   Olympic Peninsula 17

   volcanoes 13, 14

natural resources 23, 31

Pacific Ocean 7, 12, 17, 31

plants 17

population 18

Puget Sound 14, 17

recreational activities 5, 13, 23, 27, 28

Seattle 19, 20, 28, 31

   musicians from 20

   Pike Place Market 28

   Space Needle 28, 31

sports 31

   professional teams 31

Starbucks 20, 23

   founders of 20

state nickname 31

statehood 10

weather and climate 17